GO FACTS NATURAL ENVIRONMENTS
Deserts

A & C BLACK • LONDON

Deserts

contents

Copyright © 2007 Blake Publishing
Additional material © A & C Black Publishers Ltd 2008

First published in Australia by Blake Education Pty Ltd

This edition published in the UK in 2008 by
A & C Black Publishers Ltd, 38 Soho Square, London. W1D 3HB
www.acblack.com

Published by permission of Blake Publishing Pty Ltd, Leichhardt NSW, Australia.
All rights reserved. No part of this publication may be reproduced in any form
or by any means – graphic, electronical or mechanical, including photocopying,
recording, taping or information storage and retrieval systems - without the prior
written permission of the publishers.

Hardback edition
ISBN 978-1-4081-0489-7

Paperback edition
ISBN 978-1-4081-0488-0

A CIP record for this book is available from the British Library.

Author: Ian Rohr
Publisher: Katy Pike
Editor: Mark Stafford
Design and layout by The Modern Art Production Group

Image credits: p19 (all)–Mark Stafford
Printed in China by WKT Company Ltd.

This publication is produced using paper that is made from wood grown in
managed sustainable forests. It is natural, renewable and recyclable. The
logging and manufacturing processes conform to the environmental regulations
of the country of origin.

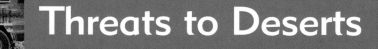

What are Deserts?

Deserts are dry places. They usually get less than 250 millimetres of rain or snow each year.

There are two main types of desert – hot and cold.

Hot deserts have lots of sand or rock and very high temperatures in summer. Hot deserts are usually at low **elevations**. The air is very dry and there are few clouds. This can cause the temperature to drop below freezing point at night.

Cold deserts have sand, rocks and ice. They are usually at high elevations, such as on **plateaux**. It is cooler at high elevations, especially in winter. Antarctica is an example of a cold desert. Instead of raining, it often snows in cold deserts.

The barrel cactus stores water.

4

Australian deserts are hot deserts.

The Gobi Desert in Mongolia is a cold desert.

HOTTEST AND COLDEST

The highest recorded temperature on Earth was 57.7 °C (135.9 °F) in Libya. The lowest temperature was −89.2 °C (-128.6 °F) in Antarctica.

Antarctica is the driest continent on Earth.

5

Deserts of the World

Each desert is different, but they all have some common features.

What a desert looks like depends on **erosion**. This is the effect of wind and water on rock. It doesn't rain much in the desert. When it does rain, it is often during storms. The rain quickly erodes rocks. Wind also erodes rocks, but it does this slowly and constantly.

Soft rocks are eroded to fine grains of sand. Winds push the sand into sand dunes. Wind storms can carry sand dunes over great distances.

Hard rocks are eroded to stones and pebbles. Nearly half of the world's deserts are plains covered with rocks and pebbles. Only 20 per cent of deserts are covered in sand.

The blue-tongued lizard lives in Australian deserts and forests.

DID YOU KNOW?

Sand dunes can sing! Some sand dunes make a loud, low rumble, even if there is no wind blowing. The sound is caused by sand sliding down the steep sides of dunes.

These rock formations in Monument Valley, USA, were created by erosion.

Kata Tjuta in Australia's Central Desert was formed by the erosion of mountains.

Sand dunes can reach 400 metres high.

7

Although deserts are dry, you can still find water in them.

Some deserts have rivers and oases.

The Nile and Colorado Rivers run through deserts. The soil soaks up some water from the rivers, and the hot weather causes a lot of water to **evaporate**.

An oasis is a place where there is a reliable water supply. An oasis forms where underground water comes to the desert surface as a **spring**. People can make oases by digging wells.

Deserts of the World

1 Antarctic Desert
2 Arabian Desert
3 Atacama Desert
4 Chihuahuan Desert
5 Gibson Desert
6 Gobi Desert
7 Great Basin Desert
8 Great Sandy Desert
9 Great Victoria Desert
10 Dasht-e Kavir Desert
11 Kalahari Desert
12 Mojave Desert
13 Namib Desert
14 Sahara Desert
15 Sonoran Desert
16 Takla Makan Desert

 hot deserts

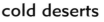 cold deserts

Desert lakes often dry out.

The Sahara

The Sahara is the largest hot desert on Earth. It covers one-third of Africa.

About one-quarter of the Sahara is made up of sand dunes and rocky plateaux. The rest of the desert is made up of gravel plains.

Plants, animals and millions of people live in the Sahara. It can get hotter than 50 °C (122 °F). The Sahara gets only 80 millimetres of rain each year. Violent sand and dust storms can blow for days. These make travel in the desert dangerous.

The Sahara has many oases, but there are long distances between them. People would not be able to live in the Sahara without oases.

Arabian camel with a decorative saddle

Some people who live in the Sahara are **nomads**.

Date palms grow at oases.

A headdress protects people from cold and blowing sand.

"Sahara" comes from the Arabic word for desert.

Desert Plants

Desert plants have special features that allow them to collect, store and conserve water.

Some desert plants have roots that cover a wide area, just below the ground. Other plants have roots that go deep underground. Mosses and lichens get water, such as **dew**, from above the ground.

prickly pear leaves

Many desert plants store water in their hollow leaves, stems or roots. These plants are called **succulents**. Plants with thick skin, and with leaves that are small or like needles, don't lose the water that they store.

Some desert plants only grow and flower after the rain falls. Seeds lying on the ground for years begin to grow when it rains. Dry grasses may look dead above ground, but their roots remain alive underground.

A saguaro cactus can grow 20 metres tall.

The spikes on a cactus prevent animals from eating the plant.

GREATEST VARIETY

The Sonoran Desert in the USA has more types of plant than any other desert in the world.

Aloe vera is a succulent.

The boab tree stores water in its trunk.

13

Desert Animals

Desert animals conserve water. They try to avoid very hot and very cold temperatures.

Animals get most of their water from the plants or animals they eat.

Reptiles store water and fat in their bodies. The Gila monster and Egyptian spiny tailed lizard save fat in their large tails. More than 100 reptile species live in the Sahara.

The fur or hair of large desert animals keeps them cool. The outer layer of a camel's coat can be 30 °C (86 °F) hotter than its body.

Some desert animals, such as the marsupial mole, burrow underground to escape extreme temperatures. It is cooler underground in hot deserts. In cold deserts, it is warmer underground.

Many hot desert animals are **nocturnal**. The addax, a nocturnal African antelope, digs a hole with its hooves and lies down in it during the hottest part of the day.

Geckos are nocturnal.

14

Penguins are desert animals.

Some desert birds, such as this roadrunner, cannot fly.

THE LARGEST
The largest scorpion in the world is the emperor scorpion from Western Africa. It can grow more than 20 centimetres long and is a popular pet.

The thorny devil drinks the dew that collects on its back.

15

A Desert Food Chain

Some desert animals eat plants. Some desert animals eat other animals.

Many desert animals are both **predators** and **prey**. Survival depends on catching food but not being caught.

1. Plants make their own food from the energy of the Sun.

2. Small animals and insects eat the seeds, leaves and flowers of these plants.

3. Small predators eat the plant eaters and other small predators.

4. Large predators eat smaller predators and plant eaters.

Desert animals are often the same colour as the ground, so predators can't see them.

Prickly pear

Jack rabbit

Golden eagle

Rattlesnake

1

2

3

4

17

Staying Cool

In a hot desert, animals stay cool underground. The soil acts as an **insulator**.

An insulator slows down or stops the movement of heat. Test for yourself how well soil works as an insulator.

What you need:

- two large tin cans
- two small tin cans
- two thermometers
- soil
- warm water
- a watch or clock
- pen and paper

Desert tortoises dig deep burrows to keep cool during the day and warm at night.

1 Put warm water and a thermometer in each of the small cans.

2 Place each small can inside a large can.

soil

3 Fill around ONE of the small cans with soil.

4 Write down the temperature of each of the thermometers. Repeat this every five minutes for 30 minutes. What is happening to the temperatures?

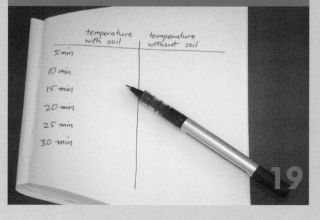

19

Threats to Deserts

Deserts are easily damaged. Mining and farms are the biggest threat to deserts.

Deserts often contain oil and iron ore. Drilling for oil and mining can harm desert environments.

Tourists can damage desert water supplies. Vehicles damage desert soils and plants.

When farms are on the edge of a desert, they can damage the fragile desert soil.

Farm animals pound the soil with their hooves. This breaks up the soil. It is then more likely to be eroded by wind and rain. When people collect firewood, or graze farm animals, they reduce the number of plants that help to bind the soil.

Goats are raised in African deserts.

The oryx antelope has been hunted to the edge of extinction.

There are many oil wells and refineries in the deserts of the Middle East.

THE HIGHEST

The highest desert in the world is the Qaidam Depression in China. It is 2600 metres above sea level.

Deserts are popular places to visit.

Some people treat deserts like rubbish dumps.

 # Desert Features

Rock

mesa (rhymes with "blazer")	a large, isolated flat-topped rock	
butte (rhymes with "mute")	a hill like a mesa, but with steeper sides	

Sand

erg (rhymes with "iceberg")	a large area of moving sand dunes	
barchan (rhymes with "barn")	a sand dune with a curved ridge	

22

Glossary

dew	drops of water that form on the ground during the night
elevation	height of land above the level of the sea
erosion	breaking down rock by wind and water
evaporate	to change from a liquid or solid to a gas
insulator	a material that electricity, heat or sound cannot go through
nocturnal	active during the night
nomad	a person who moves around rather than living in one place
plateau	a large, flat area of land, high above sea level
predator	an animal that hunts, kills and eats other animals
prey	an animal that is hunted and killed by another animal
spring	a place where water naturally flows from the ground
succulent	a plant that stores water in its leaves and stem

Index